The Story of Science

# The Wonders of Biodiversity

## by Roy A. Gallant

**BENCHMARK BOOKS**

MARSHALL CAVENDISH
NEW YORK

Series Editor: Roy A. Gallant

Series Consultants:

LIFE SCIENCES
Dr. Edward J. Kormondy
Chancellor and Professor of Biology (retired)
University of Hawaii-Hilo/West Oahu

PHYSICAL SCIENCES
Dr. Jerry LaSala
Department of Physics
University of Southern Maine

Benchmark Books
Marshall Cavendish
99 White Plains Road
Tarrytown, NY 10591-9001

Library of Congress Cataloging-in-Publication Data
Gallant, Roy A.
        The wonders of biodiversity / by Roy A. Gallant.
        p. cm. — (The story of science)
Summary: Discusses the many different life forms that have existed on
Earth, their importance, and how they have changed over time.
Includes bibliographical references and index.
ISBN 0-7614-1427-4
        1. Biological diversity—Juvenile literature. [1. Biological
diversity.] I. Title. II. Series.
    QH541.15.B56 G35 2002      333.95'11—dc21      2002000916

Photo research by Linda Sykes Picture Research, Hilton Head, SC
Diagrams on pp. 21, 27, 29, 39 by Ian Worpole
Cover: Cosmos Blank/Photo Researchers
Photo credits: Jim Brandenberg/Minden Pictures: 1, 44; Frans Lanting/Minden Pictures: 7, 66;
E. R. Degginger/Animals, Animals: 9 (top); George Bryce/Animals, Animals: 9 (middle);
Patti Murray/Animals, Animals: 9 (bottom); John Cancalosi/Peter Arnold: 10; Dr. Kari
Ounatmaa/Science Photo Library/Photo Researchers: 15 (top), 15 (bottom); Dan
Cheatham/DRK Photo: 16; Kevin Morris/Corbis: 19; Andrew Syred/Photo Researchers:
22 (top); M. I. Walker/Photo Researchers: 22 (middle); David Phillips/Photo Researchers:
22 (bottom); George Bernard/Earth Scenes: 26; Roger de la Harpe/Earth Scenes: 31;
C. Allan Morgan/Peter Arnold: 32; Mark Stouffer/Animals, Animals: 34; Tom McHugh/Photo
Researchers: 35; Carr Clifton/Minden Pictures: 36, 40 (top), 41; Michael Giannechini/Photo
Researchers: 40 (bottom); Yva Momatiuk-John Eastciott/Minden Pictures: 43 (top);
S. J. Krasemann/Peter Arnold: 43 (bottom); Tom Bean/DRK Photo: 45; Marie Read/Earth
Scenes: 47; M. Harvey/DRK Photo: 49; Gerry Ellis/Minden Pictures: 52–53; Julian Hume: 55;
Academy of Natural Sciences of Philadelphia/Corbis: 61; Michael Fogden/DRK Photo: 64; Kelvin
Aitken/Peter Arnold: 67; Anup Shah/DRK Photo: 73 (left); Tom and Pat Leeson/DRK Photo: 73
(right).

Cover design by Bob O'Brien

Printed in Hong Kong

6 5 4 3 2 1

For Josh and Luke

*In our generation we, the only species on Earth with the mental capacity to reason, will see the virtual disappearance of contiguous tropical forests and probably the extermination of more than 20 percent of the diversity of life on Earth, and we humans will have caused it.*

*—Terry L. Erwin,*
*Biologist, Smithsonian Institution,*
*Washington, D.C.*

# Contents

# One

# Beetles, Bacteria, and Biodiversity

For biologist Terry L. Erwin of the Smithsonian Institution in Washington, D.C., few things bring more satisfaction than the hushed rain of a thousand beetles and other insects tumbling down out of the leafy rooftop, the *canopy*, of a tropical rain forest.

To collect their booty of insects, Erwin and his students first unfold sheets and suspend them just above the forest floor. Next they point a fogging gun skyward and spray a cloud of biodegradable insecticide up into the leaves, branches, and vines of the canopy. Moments later the shower of insects begins. After two or three such foggings Erwin and his workers pack up their catch and head back to camp. Their

*Boxes of beetles fill biologist Terry Erwin's Smithsonian Institution laboratory. To study insect diversity in tropical forests, he and his students shake-fog the forest canopy and wait anxiously for a rain of beetles that fall into collecting sheets stretched out just above the forest floor.*

next job is to separate the insects into groups of known and unknown species. One such fogging in a Peruvian rain forest flushed out more than 650 beetle species. To date, scientists have classified, or named, more than 350,000 species of beetles alone, so diverse are these six-legged critters. Of all known insect species, almost half are beetles. Of the total number of plant and animal species we share the planet with—anywhere from 10 million to 100 million—biologists

have classified a mere 1.75 million. And each year they add about another 15,000 to the list.

## A Symphony of Species

The study of fossil animals and plants shows how life forms have evolved over the millennia by reacting to changes in the environment. Some populations have adapted to new conditions brought on by climate change and evolved into new species. Others have not, and their species have become extinct. Of the billions of species that have come and gone since life first arose on this planet nearly four billion years ago, more than 99 percent have become extinct. We are just beginning to understand the significance of the astonishing diversity of past and present life forms on Earth and how their often bewildering and always beautiful variety weaves a supportive web that makes life possible for our own species.

Life's infinite variety sometimes seems uncanny. There are plants, such as the Venus flytrap, the lethal lollipop, and the pitcher plant that trap and "eat" insects. The nonpoisonous king snake has color bands that make it look like a poisonous coral snake. Predators are fooled, and so the king snake enjoys a survival advantage. There are moths and caterpillars with color patterns resembling enormous false eyes that usually keep hungry birds away. And there are thousands of costumes that tend to make a wide variety of animals, such as ground-nesting birds, invisible to predators. The bottom-feeding flounder fish, for example, can actually change its color pattern so that it is often impossible to see against the pattern of the seafloor. All such examples of mimicry, or look-alike markings, are adaptations that give their owners a more than even chance of going unseen and not ending up on some other animal's dinner plate.

A nonpoisonous king snake (above) mimics the color pattern of the poisonous eastern coral snake (at top). Predators shy away from the harmless king snake, fooled into thinking its bite spells death. False eyes, which are mere color patterns on the head end of this swallowtail butterfly caterpillar (right), and on the wings of certain moths, trick predators into thinking that an equally large mouth awaits them if they strike.

*Cryptic coloration in this white-tailed ptarmigan is an adaptation that helps hide the bird from predators. Those species well adapted to their environment tend to survive and so produce offspring equally well adapted. This principle of survival is called natural selection and is the engine of evolution.*

A truly remarkable example of adaptation is found in a small, green, African clawed frog with black and yellow speckles. When the frog is even slightly injured, a white fluid begins to ooze out of its skin and coats the injured area. The ooze is a combination of chemicals from the frog's natural medicine cabinet that kills almost all known bacteria and so prevents infection. The discovery of this frog's remarkable ability to fight infections with its own homemade antibiotic mixture may be important to our own health.

For example, practitioners of Chinese folk medicine have long depended on the chemical secretions of toads to treat open sores and dog bites. It turns out that all frogs and toads give off fluids that have antibiotic powers. So do beetles,

A herd of cows, a colony of ants, a flock of geese, or any other healthy population is suited to, or adapted to, its environment. A Gila monster, for example, is physically adapted to the heat and dryness of the desert. The population could not survive in the Arctic any more than a polar bear could survive in the desert.

# Diversity and Adaptation

Over time, the environment changes, as it has ever since Earth formed some 4.6 billion years ago. Ice ages come and go. New mountains are thrust up and change the local climate. Swamps and inland seas dry up. Glaciers melt. All such changes force new conditions on the plants and animals living there. Sometimes such changes are so severe that no individual members of a population can survive, and the population dies out. In other cases, when the change is less severe, certain individuals that are fitter than the others are able to survive. A squirrel with a thicker coat of hair might be better able to survive a series of especially cold winters than a squirrel with only a thin coat. A moth with wing colors that make it especially hard for birds to find is better protected than moths that are less well camouflaged. Such "favored" individuals in a population are produced randomly, or by chance, in a process called *mutation.*

Mutation is a change in a plant's or an animal's genes that may make the plant or animal different in one or more important ways from its parents. One

*Continued on page 12*

*Continued from page 11*

puppy in a litter may have one brown eye and one blue eye, although all of its brothers and sisters have eyes that are both the same color. X rays and certain other forms of radiation can cause mutations. Even though most mutations are harmful, occasionally one just happens to turn out beneficial, as in the case of the squirrel with an especially thick coat of hair. When that happens, we say that the individual with the mutation is well adapted to the new environment. Those individuals that are well adapted and survive may then pass on their special adaptation to their offspring. Those without the new adaptation are more likely to die before reproducing.

Gradually the population rebuilds as its new and fitter individuals produce offspring with the beneficial mutation. Those offspring, like their parents, are different from those that were unable to survive the environmental change. This is basically how the process called evolution changes populations and produces new species of plants and animals that account for the never-ending process of biodiversity.

wasps, ants, termites, bees, the nectar of certain plants, the silk of spiders, and who knows how many millions of other critters we have not even come to know yet. So the more we can learn about these marvelously diverse animals and plants and the medicinal chemicals they produce naturally, the better off we may be in addressing our own health problems.

Our overuse of antibiotic medicines to treat human ailments nearly always makes the harmful bacteria we hope to kill increasingly resistant to our antibiotic drugs. Through adaptation, bacteria "learn" how to become immune to our drugs.

The tropical rain forests, with their nearly limitless arsenal of known and unknown animals and plants, are a treasure house of medicines that we are just beginning to discover. Steroids, penicillin, morphine, and aspirin are only four products of Western medicine that have their origins in the natural world. From shark's liver to tree bark, the incredible biodiversity of nature offers us medicinal benefits we have never even dreamed of.

A remarkable thing about adaptation is how quickly it can take place, both over spans of geologic time and in our own clock time. Well into the twentieth century, biologists assumed that evolution was a process of slow and gradual change, one needing tens or hundreds of millions of years. More recently, however, paleontologists Niles Eldredge and Stephen Jay Gould have shown that evolution sometimes surges ahead, one animal or plant group evolving into something quite different in only a few million years. Their evidence is the frequent appearance in the fossil record of new species with no apparent ancestors that they resemble.

## Adaptation in a Test Tube

Populations of bacteria are examples of small organisms that adapt astonishingly quickly—sometimes virtually overnight—to new ecosystems. The English biologist Paul Rainey, who studies diversity among bacteria, has worked with one species, named *Pseudomonas fluorescens*, that grows on plants and in the soil. Like most bacteria, this one increases its numbers by dividing every twenty minutes. Start with one bacterium, and twenty minutes later there are two. Twenty minutes after that there are four. After a day or so, that one original bacterium has given rise to a population in the billions.

Rainey once grew a colony of *P. fluorescens* bacteria in a test tube containing a nourishing broth. He started his experiment with a single bacterium and sealed the test tube to prevent other bacteria from entering. He then put the tube aside and did not disturb it for four days. Imagine his surprise when at the end of that time he examined the colony and found several different kinds of bacteria instead of millions of faithful copies of his original single *P. fluorescens*. One distinct type was growing in the upper levels of the broth, where there was a rich supply of oxygen. A different type had evolved near the bottom of the tube, where there was less oxygen. A still different type had taken up life as a ring of growth, like a bathtub ring. Finally, there was a matlike growth of a fourth type at the surface of the broth, along the side of the tube.

Different conditions within the test tube created different small *habitats*, each one unique. Competition for living space, combined with the ability of bacteria to adapt to the test tube's different habitats, had accounted for the resulting biodiversity. A vigorous shaking of the test tube would destroy the varied habitats, and with them the variety of bacteria. In a small way, it would be like shoveling an entire tropical rain forest into a giant jar, shaking the jar vigorously, and then spilling it all back out. Countless species would be destroyed, while countless others would take up a new life in the many new nooks and crannies of the altered environment. While those species adapted to the altered conditions, the environment itself would react and change even more in response to the ways its inhabitants carried on their lives.

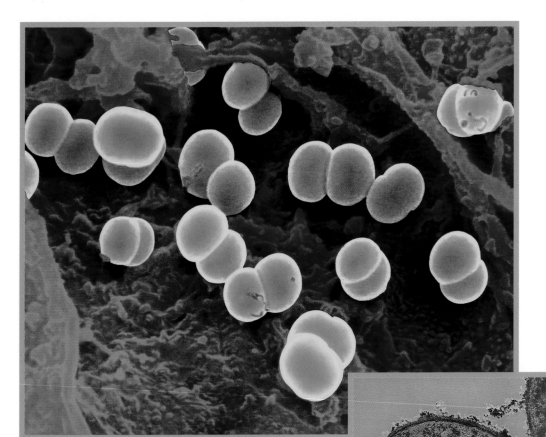

Biodiversity abounds among the fast-reproducing bacteria. The paired green bacteria shown above (Enterococci) normally live in our intestines. Some are harmless while others infect wounds and still others can cause food poisoning. The bacterium at right (Streptococcus) is in the process of dividing into two new organisms. Streptococci live in our noses and throats and are a common cause of throat infections.

*The hollow thorns of the acacia provide a home for ants while tender leaf tips provide food. The ants drive predators away from the plant and trim away other plant growth that threatens the acacia with unwanted shade. There are many such helpful plant and animal relationships in nature, called mutualism.*

# Two Plant–Animal Relationships

***The Long-tongued Fly and the Orchid*** An example of how diversity among one group of organisms can influence diversity among another group can be seen in a long-tongued fly of southwestern Africa and the nectar-producing flowers on which the fly feeds. The flowers—certain irises, orchids, and geraniums—have especially deep cavities where the nectar is stored. Only the long-tongued fly is able to reach the nectar. As it feeds, it collects pollen on its body, and carries the pollen to other flowers where it rubs off and fertilizes the plants. In this way, these plants have come to depend on the long-tongued fly for their well-being. Without the fly, plant species might not reproduce and without the flowers as a rich store of nectar, the long-tongued fly might face food problems. The extinction or depletion of one or both species could change the local environment's biodiversity in unknown ways.

***A Thorn Plant and Its Ants*** The acacia thorn plant has tender leaf tips that ants cut off and use as food for their young. The ants also chew a window opening near the tip of a thorn and use the interior as living space. So the plant provides the ants with both food and shelter. In return, the ants meet two essential needs of the acacia. They patrol the acacia day and night, biting and stinging insect invaders that try to use the plant as food. (The acacia, unlike many other plants, lacks a chemical defense system to repel harmful insects.) In addition the ants make sure that the acacia gets the full sunlight it needs for healthy growth. Whenever another plant grows too close to the acacia and threatens it with shade, the ants cut through the trespassing plant's soft stem and cut off its leaves. Deprived of acacia leaf tips, the ants might starve to death. Deprived of the ants, the acacia might die, too.

# Two

# Critters Galore: What They Are

## The Age of Bacteria

To realize the power of the diversity of Earth's early organisms, we have to turn the geological clock back about three billion years. We could not have breathed the air then. It was largely carbon dioxide, carbon monoxide, and hydrogen, with hardly any oxygen. The landscape was a kaleidoscope of brilliantly colored mats of bacteria—scum clinging to rocks, coating the surfaces of ponds, and stuck to riverbanks. Tacky, threadlike crowds of bacteria—blue, red, yellow, orange—carpeted the land from horizon to horizon.

The many forms of bacteria most likely dominated the planet for its first few billion years of life. Some differed from others in their ability to thrive amid especially high temperatures. Other groups

*Rainbows of colorful bacteria adorn the hot springs of Yellowstone National Park. Marvels of adaptation, the bacteria serve as natural thermometers because those of certain colors live within only certain ranges of water temperature.*

needed lots of sunlight, and others that got on nicely in the scum of lake bottoms with little or no light. Some groups adapted to life in salty water, while still others lived only in freshwater.

As Earth became increasingly populated by the rapidly growing bacteria, their chemical interaction with their surroundings was bound to change the environment in many ways. For example, the waste gases given off by a large group of bacteria might have accumulated in amounts that became poisonous to some groups. These bacteria would have died, leaving those able to cope with the new environment. This process is called natural selection.

Among the other environmental crises that bacteria had to face during the Age of Bacteria were drought or changes in the air quality brought on by volcanoes that vented vast clouds of dust and noxious gases. But where successful mutations abounded, new populations arose fully adapted to these new environmental conditions. Populations not so adapted died out.

# Poisonous Oxygen Fouls the Air

Among that seemingly endless carpet of bacteria, some species took in ready-made food from the environment. Others made their own food by using sunlight to combine carbon dioxide from the air with hydrogen from water in the soil, a process called *photosynthesis*. As they did, they brought on the greatest natural "catastrophe" that Earth has ever experienced. That natural disaster was the introduction into the environment of a gas that was poisonous to nearly all cells living at the time—oxygen. Oxygen, so precious to most organisms living today, is given off as a "waste" gas during photosynthesis.

As more and more oxygen kept entering the air, trouble started. Unless an organism's structure protects it from oxygen, it will be poisoned by the gas. Free oxygen quickly combines with and destroys living matter. It breaks down vitamins. It destroys proteins and destroys a cell's protective membrane sac that holds the cell together, killing the cell instantly. Many populations of bacteria were wiped out by this new gas. But those that had taken up life in mudflats and swamp bottoms avoided the gas and survived. Such bacteria have remained unchanged through the ages and are wildly successful to this day. They are the *cyanobacteria* that form the scum on swimming pools and that coat shower curtains. Certain other bacteria learned to live with oxygen—they even came to depend on it.

Life would never be the same again. The stage was set for those simplest life forms to evolve into complex cells, then into colonies of cells, and then into the overwhelming variety of animals and plants that have come and gone over the hundreds of millions of years of Earth's history.

There is a good reason for dwelling on bacteria as much as we have. In all of biology, nowhere do we find better examples

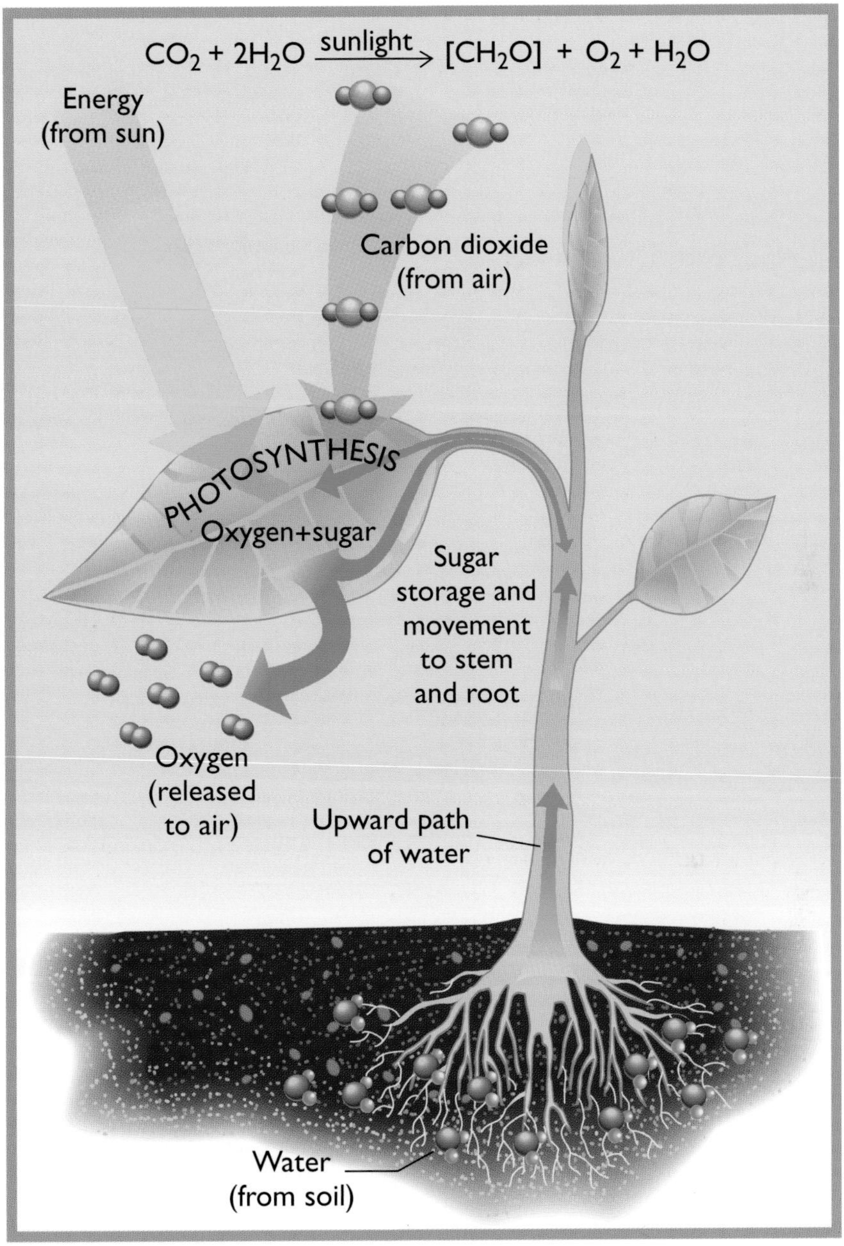

$$CO_2 + 2H_2O \xrightarrow{\text{sunlight}} [CH_2O] + O_2 + H_2O$$

Energy
(from sun)

Carbon dioxide
(from air)

PHOTOSYNTHESIS

Oxygen+sugar

Sugar
storage and
movement
to stem
and root

Oxygen
(released
to air)

Upward path
of water

Water
(from soil)

*In photosynthesis, carbon dioxide drawn in from the air by the leaves of green plants is combined with water drawn from the soil and produces sugar and oxygen. These chemical reactions are powered by sunlight. The sugar formed during photosynthesis is the basic fuel of all forms of life on Earth.*

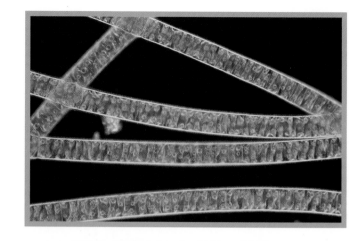

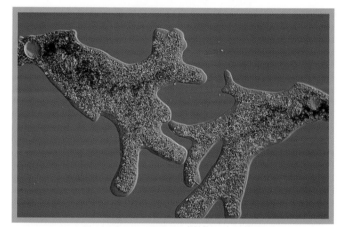

Many kinds of single-cell organisms more complex than bacteria eventually took up life in water. Among them were (from top to bottom) Spirogyra, a green alga that forms slimy threads in stagnant water; amoebas, formless organisms that move about by flowing their cell material into extensions called "false feet"; and Euglena, which has a light-sensitive red-spot "eye" and a whiplike tail that acts as an outboard motor for propulsion.

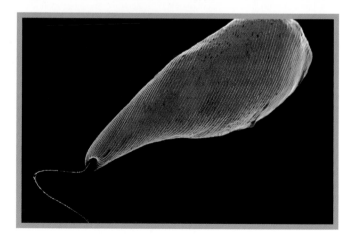

of populations of organisms, small or large, adapting to environmental change as quickly or as thoroughly. And nowhere else do we find organisms as able to alter their environment—from creating an environment of infection in a cut finger to altering Earth's atmosphere by starting the oxygen revolution about 3 to 2.5 billion years ago. Those ideas are at the heart of biodiversity: the ability of populations of organisms to bring about changes in the environment and how they adapt to those changes or perish.

Following the Age of Bacteria, many kinds of single-celled organisms evolved. Certain of those organisms joined in partnerships that gave rise to colonies of cells. By some 700 million years ago there were numerous soft-bodied animals living in globelike and wormlike forms in the seas. Because they were soft-bodied, their fossils in sandstone show few details of their structure. It is likely that early relatives of starfish and sea urchins also lived in those seas. While we do not have as much evidence of these soft-bodied creatures as we do later organisms, it appears that they lived in the time between the colonies of cells and later complex organisms—plants and animals with hard parts that became such abundant and perfect fossils 200 million years later.

## Spitting Spiders and Glue Worms

In their book, *Wild Solutions,* authors Andrew Beattie and Paul Ehrlich describe many curious adaptations of animals. Some of these involve using glue for survival. One creature, the tiny velvet worm, an unlikely predator, captures and eats insects. Its offensive weapons are a pair of "glue guns," one on each side of its mouth. When it comes within range of an ant, for instance, it fires jets of glue in the form of threads that entangle the ant beyond escape. The worm then eats the ant at leisure. A spider that also lives on insect delicacies similarly spits threads of glue that entangle a hapless and helpless mosquito, which the spider promptly eats. And there are bacteria that glue themselves to their rock homes in the shallows near ocean shores.

There are thousands upon thousands of other equally inventive and curious adaptations among animals and plants. We study them not only because we are curious about these behaviors that help make this or that species able to survive in the jungle of "eat or be eaten," but because we may learn from those behaviors or the chemical agents involved. As with medicinal drugs that we have developed from certain tropical rain forest plants, it may turn out that those bacteria or velvet worms or spitting spiders may teach us about new adhesives that could be used in many difficult applications. For example, they may show us the way toward adhesives that could be used in underwater repairs of ships' hulls, or in the repair of organs such as our liver or other soft body parts that are difficult to patch or stitch.

The actual number of plant and animal species in the world is unknown. While we are more familiar with the large creatures of the world—whales, elephants, and giant redwoods—it's the really small species that are large in number and the most interesting. Scoop up a pinch of forest soil and examine it under a microscope. You will soon see that about half the tiny grains of soil are not lifeless bits of matter but are small organisms slowly creeping around. There may be nearly a million species of bacteria in the world and a million and a half of fungi. A bit larger are those single-celled plants known as algae, of which there may be nearly half a million species. And the single-celled animals called protozoa may number 200,000 species. Then come even larger critters, including mites and tiny worms that may contain another million species. And then there is the staggering variety of beetles—at present we know of only about half a million species. According to Beattie and Ehrlich, the bark beetle— not much larger than a pinhead—is home to at least three species of mites, four species of roundworms, seven species of bacteria, and three species of fungi. Life abounds!

On the scale of decreasing diversity and species numbers, after the nearly one million known species of insects come trees and other flowering plants, of which there may be 320,000 species. Next come 200,000 species of clams, mussels, oysters, and other mollusks, followed by 150,000 species of crustaceans, which include lobsters, crabs, and crayfish. Fish species are still fewer, with about 35,000 species. At the far end of the scale of animal species diversity and numbers are those that are the least diverse but the most familiar to us—birds, with nearly 10,000 species; reptiles, with nearly 8,000 species; mammals, with about 4,800 species; and amphibians, also with almost 4,800 species.

As with the tiny bark beetle, all animals and trees are home to a variety of other critters. A tree may be home to a parasitic vine, which uses the tree only for support, or to the strangler fig, which at first uses a host tree for support but eventually kills the tree by competing with it for nutrients. At the same time the tree may be home to one or more bird species, a host of insects that the birds feed on, fungi, worms, lizards, and even mammals. Each animal or plant species may be adapted to live on that species of tree alone. The silkworm lives on and eats only the leaves of the mulberry. If it lays its eggs on another kind of plant, the emerging caterpillar "worm" will refuse to eat and will starve to death.

# Organizing the Natural World

Scientists try to keep track of the infinite variety of plants and animals by naming them and placing them in groups in meaningful ways. In the 1700s several scientists developed schemes to relate the bewildering variety of plants and animals. Among them were the French scientists Georges Buffon and Georges Cuvier, and most notably the Swedish naturalist and physician Carl von Linné, who lived from 1707 to 1778. All three based their systems of grouping, or classifying, plants and animals on an organism's structure or anatomy. Von Linné's system is the one used today. That branch of science dealing with the classification of organisms is known as *taxonomy*, or systematics.

*Carl von Linné, the Swedish naturalist who is most credited with developing the system by which science classifies organisms in that branch of science called taxonomy, or systematics.*

A particular kind of plant or animal is given two names from Latin words, or words that are latinized. For example, modern human beings are classified *Homo sapiens*, from the Latin words meaning "man" and "wise." An earlier human type was called *Homo erectus*, meaning "upright man." The first name in this double-name system designates a broad group of human types, and that group is called a *genus*. The second name designates a smaller or more specific group called a *species*. Your pet dog belongs to the genus *Canis* and the species *familiaris*. We can write the name as *Canis familiaris*, or abbreviate it *C. familiaris*. Notice that a genus-species name is always written in italic type and the genus name begins with a capital letter. Von Linné thought so highly of his classification system that he latinized his own name to *Linnaeus carolus*.

Moving upward in the Linnaean classification system, your pet dog becomes a member of larger and larger groups. At the genus level he is joined by coyotes; at the family level by lions and foxes; at the order level by bears; at the class level by deer and all other mammals; and at the highest level—kingdom—by all other animals.

In all there are five kingdoms—*Animalia* (animals), *Plantae* (plants), *Fungi* (mushrooms, for example), *Protista* (golden algae and diatoms, for example), and *Monera* (true bacteria and blue-green algae, for example). Von Linné did not know of all these groups. But as our knowledge about biodiversity has grown, the classification system has had to change, and it will continue to change in the future as new species are discovered.

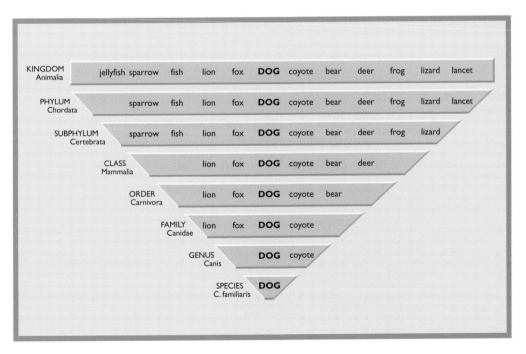

# Three

# Critters Galore: Where They Live

## Spaceship Earth

You live in a spaceship, although you probably don't realize it. Spaceship *Earth* travels around the Sun at an average speed of about 67,000 miles (107,800 kilometers) an hour. But we can speed things up a bit if we add the Sun's speed around the hub of the galaxy, which is about 468,000 miles (753,200 kilometers) an hour. Those two speeds combined give spaceship *Earth* a velocity of about 535,000 miles (861,000 kilometers) an hour. At that speed, it takes our planet 240 million years—called a *cosmic year*—to make one circuit of the galaxy and return to its starting point. By the end of that very long year its starting point doesn't even exist anymore because all the stars have moved to different locations.

*A typical food chain has producers (grass, trees, and shrubs). It also contains herbivores (grass- and leaf-eating animals), and carnivores (meat-eating animals) that eat the herbivores. Eventually all members of a food chain die and their remains are broken down as nutrients by fungi and other decomposers of the soil. The nutrients are then recycled again and again.*

During that very long time our spaceship has not had to take on any food supplies, breathable air, or any other materials from the outside to maintain a planetwide environment friendly enough to support its billions of life forms. Nor has the planet had to rid itself of waste matter since all wastes have been recycled and converted into clean air, clean water, and food. In effect, planet Earth is what biologists call a *closed ecological system*, one that can run virtually forever by continuously replenishing and maintaining itself. We have imported only one thing—solar energy. That energy, in the form of sunlight, drives the chemical machinery of photosynthesis. Photosynthesis enables the leaves of green plants—grass, corn, wheat, fruit trees—to produce the oxygen we breathe and to manufacture glucose, the sugar that feeds the world.

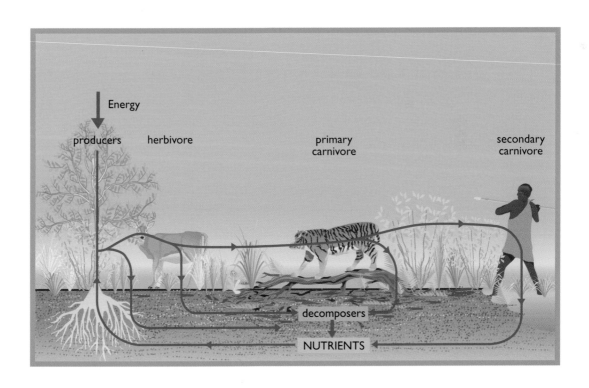

# How an Ecosystem Works

Over the nearly four billion years since life began on this planet, the chemicals of life have been endlessly reused and exchanged by plants, animals, the soil, the oceans, and the atmosphere. Some of those chemicals are oxygen, nitrogen, carbon, phosphorus, hydrogen, and sulfur. All the chemicals that make up your body were once part of a dinosaur, a whale, a lump of coal, or some other form of matter, and they will one day in the distant future be used again by still other organisms in *ecosystems* very different from your own.

There are many kinds of ecosystems, each with distinctive communities of organisms living together and depending on one another and their surroundings for nourishment and shelter. Let's consider one ecosystem in some detail and describe some rather interesting adaptations of a few of the plants and animals that live there.

# Animal Life in a Desert Ecosystem

Many people imagine deserts as relatively lifeless places with only some cactus plants and an occasional snake crawling into the shade of a large rock to escape the fierce heat of the desert sand. But if you've spent much time in desert country, such as that of the American Southwest, you know that a desert ecosystem is home to numerous species of plants and animals that have adapted to the harsh conditions there. Even a sand dune habitat can be home to as many as thirty different species. While certain plants grow at the dune's surface, burrowing wasps may live inside the dune. Cottontail rabbits, meadow voles, grasshoppers, and termites often make their homes in a dead and decaying tree buried in the dune.

You probably have hopped around to avoid burning your feet on a hot sandy beach in the summertime. Although the

*Gigantic or dwarf, inland or by the shore, seemingly lifeless sand dunes harbor complex communities of plant and animal life, each species uniquely adapted to living in such harsh environments. This enormous dune is near Sossusviei, Nambia, in Africa.*

air temperature might be 90°F (32°C), the surface sand is a sizzling 120°F (49°C). The temperature difference often is even greater in a desert environment.

Although some plants thrive in such heat, animals rarely can, at least not for long. Most of Earth's animals—including toads, fishes, snakes, salamanders, and insects—are unable to control their body temperature, which rises and falls right along with the temperature of their surroundings. As the air around these *cold-blooded* animals heats up during the day or cools down at night, the animal's body temperature changes accordingly. Since these animals can't regulate their temperature, they must stay out of the sun during the hottest part of the day.

Mammals, which include humans, dogs, mice, and rabbits, do not have this problem. Neither do birds. They are *warm-blooded* animals and can maintain a constant body temperature. They can shiver to warm up or sweat or pant to cool down. But even warm-blooded animals may have trouble maintaining their body temperature when their surroundings become unusually hot or cold. Overheating can cause a person to faint or even to die.

Hopping about on that sandy beach, you probably dug in your toes to feel the refreshingly cool sand just a few inches down. A kangaroo rat and other desert animals escape the heat by going below the surface. They make their burrow homes a foot or so beneath the surface, where it is comfortably cool by

*Well adapted to its desert biome home, this kangaroo rat is a model of water conservation. It uses water from the food it eats so economically that it urinates in the form of dry pellets, with no water needed at all.*

day and warm by night. Furthermore, these desert-burrowing animals usually are active only during the early morning, in the evening, or at night when they can avoid the intense heat.

But heat isn't the only challenge desert animals face. They also need to deal with a lack of moisture. Most of them have built-in ways of conserving water. Kangaroo rats of the Sonoran, Mojave, and Colorado Deserts get the water they need from the seeds and vegetation they eat. Their urine contains so little water that it turns into solid pellets when it comes in contact with the air. The kangaroo rat is a model of water conservation.

Another of the kangaroo rat's adaptations to desert life is its ability to jump along in 8-foot (2.4-meter) leaps at a speed of nearly 15 miles (24 kilometers) an hour. The fur around a kangaroo rat's toes turns its feet into "sandshoes" that prevent it from sinking into the sand. Its long tail helps the animal keep its balance as it bounds along, fleeing from enemies such as a sidewinder rattlesnake or a kit fox.

You often see clusters of tiny funnel-shaped pits in the desert floor. They are traps dug by insects called ant lions that lie in wait at the bottom of the pits. When an ant or other insect tumbles down the loose sand walls, the ant lion grabs it with powerful jaws and pushes into the sand where it paralyzes the unlucky guest with a poisonous fluid released from its mouth. It then relaxes and eats its victim. Other insect predators of the desert include tiger beetles that skip over the sand in pursuit of other insect prey, robberflies that suck the body juices out of their victims, and jumping spiders that hunt like cats.

Deserts of the American Southwest also have a type of toad called a spadefoot. These animals spend ten months of the year underground, coming to the surface only during the brief summer rains. As the water wets the desert landscape and trickles into

*Funnel-shaped pit traps dug by ant lions wait for any careless insect to tumble into the trap and into the jaws of the ant lion waiting below.*

the ground, an entire population of spadefoots suddenly appears. For a few days they occupy every pool and puddle made by the rain, and their mating calls fill the air.

The toads mate and the females lay their eggs. Within two weeks the eggs have hatched and the pollywogs have developed into adults capable of living on dry land. Usually the young grow up just before the remaining pools are dried away by the heat. The toads then dig their way into the desert floor for another long period before the rains come again.

## Plant Life in a Desert Ecosystem

Like desert animals, desert plants have adaptations for using water conservatively. The thin "spines" of some cactus plants are actually leaves shaped to reduce water loss through evaporation. The fleshy stems of cactus plants store water for use in times of need.

For most of the year the branches of the night-blooming cereus cactus are drab green-brown twigs. However, when winter rains come, small green buds appear and continue to grow through May. Then on one, and only one, night when the humidity and temperature are just right, the buds of all the cereus plants in an area burst open and reveal a beautiful, richly scented flower the size of your fist. As if by magic, sphinx moths appear, flying from one flower to another and pollinating the plants. This is the plants' one night of glory. Just before dawn the flowers wither, revealing a red seedpod. By sunrise the plants once again show only their drab green-brown color.

*Seemingly strange adaptations abound among plants and animals alike. The desert cereus cactus waits for conditions to be exactly right before its flowers bloom—on only one night of the year, but long enough for sphinx moths to pollinate its flower.*

When greasewood plants grow on or around a broad sand dune, they often are so evenly spaced that it seems as though they were planted that way, but they weren't. This spacing is a result of the plant's special adaptation to a climate where water is scarce. The greasewood plant puts out shallow roots that form a 25-foot (8-meter) wide circle around the plant. This root system gives off a harmful chemical that prevents the roots of other greasewood plants from growing too close. As a result, each plant is able to grow an extensive root system that collects the water it needs, while at the same time preventing neighboring plants from competing for water.

The saguaro cactus has a deep taproot that grows straight down, in addition to an extensive network of horizontal roots not far beneath the surface. The plant's horizontal roots, which may fan out more than 75 feet (23 meters), collect summer rainwater.

*The saguaro cactus is another marvel of adaptation. It has a fine root system that fans out close to the surface, collects rain, and sends the water for storage into the plant's deep tap root, which also firmly anchors the plant.*

That water is then stored in the taproot and used during times of water shortage. The taproot also firmly anchors the plant.

Some dune plants, such as the smoke bush, have tough seeds that need exactly the right amount of moisture to sprout. Sometimes, the seeds lie on the ground for years. Eventually, during a fierce storm, the rushing water of flash floods picks up the seeds and dashes them against the sand and rocks. Some become trapped in crannies in the streambed, and water soaks into the seeds through cracks created during their violent journey. Only then do the seeds germinate and new plants begin to grow.

Together, dune plants and animals form a dune *community*. The creatures living in any ecosystem community depend on each other, much as the people in a city or town do. Desert plants provide seeds as food for kangaroo rats and certain other animals. The plants, in turn, depend on the animals of the community. The seeds of some dune plants cannot sprout until they are collected by a sand rat. The rats carry the seeds into their dune burrows, where they eat some and store the rest. Some of these stored seeds sprout, push up through the sand, and grow along the surface of the dune.

The location of a sand dune—in a desert, beside a lake, by the seashore—determines the kinds of creatures that make up an ecological community. For example, strong winds often blow insects living in and near the Indiana dunes out into Lake Michigan where they drown. However, their bodies are carried back to shore and serve as a source of food for dune birds of the community.

So, as with any ecosystem, the biodiversity of a desert community is what keeps the community healthy and thriving. Reduce the biodiversity, and the productivity of the community declines. Animals die, and plants wither away. What was once a thriving assembly of plants and animals exchanging matter and energy becomes, for a while at least, a heap of lifeless, shifting sand.

# Four

# Major Ecosystems

In the previous chapter, we considered deserts as ecosystems, although we spoke mainly about the hot sandy desert region of the American Southwest. But there are other desert ecosystems, each with its own characteristic mix of plant and animal communities and each quite different from the home of the kangaroo rat and sidewinder. There is the cold Great Basin desert region of the American Northwest where jackrabbits and pronghorn antelope live. And there is the rocky Negev Desert of Israel where camels have a remarkable adaptation for water conservation and a tolerance for a large range in body temperature. But there are other very different and larger-scale ecosystems, called *biomes*, with still greater arrays of biodiversity. If you traveled by car from

*Earth has large-scale ecosystems called biomes. Among them are the great north woods, also called the north coniferous forest biome. Other biomes include tropical rain forests, grasslands, mid-latitude deciduous forests, deserts, and the tundra.*

Canada's far north southward to the Equator, you would pass through several biomes and could not help but notice how the land and its animal and plant populations change.

## Tundra

The tundra, meaning "marshy plain," stretches around the globe south of the arctic ice and down to about latitude 60 degrees north, a biome that includes northern Canada, northern Greenland, Iceland, Sweden, Norway, Finland, the northern half of Russia, and nearly all of Alaska. Many regions of tundra lack large trees and instead have widespread lichen growth including reindeer moss, grasses, dwarf trees and shrubs, and spongy and hummocky soil that is poorly drained and underlaid by permanently frozen ground called *permafrost*. The highest tundra temperatures average below 50°F (10°C).

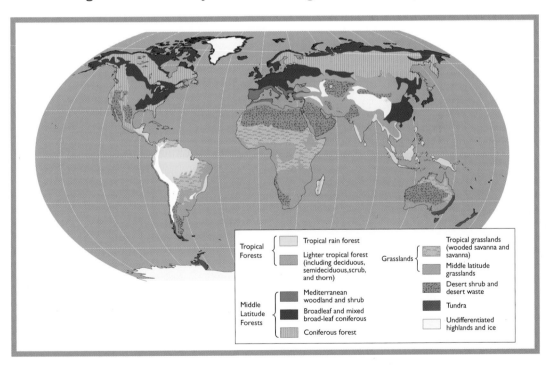

| | | | |
|---|---|---|---|
| Tropical Forests | Tropical rain forest | Grasslands | Tropical grasslands (wooded savanna and savanna) |
| | Lighter tropical forest (including deciduous, semideciduous, scrub, and thorn) | | Middle latitude grasslands |
| | | | Desert shrub and desert waste |
| Middle Latitude Forests | Mediterranean woodland and shrub | | Tundra |
| | Broadleaf and mixed broad-leaf coniferous | | Undifferentiated highlands and ice |
| | Coniferous forest | | |

*Most of Alaska is tundra biome typified by grasses, dwarf trees and shrubs, and hummocky soil called permafrost. The southern limit of the tundra is about 60 degrees north. The scene here is Alaska's Denali National Park and Preserve.*

The main tundra animals are caribou (also called reindeer), musk oxen, arctic hares, voles, and lemmings, all of which are plant eaters. The meat eaters include the arctic fox and wolves. Reptiles and amphibians are scarce. In summer the mosquitoes and blackflies are fierce. Birds include longspurs, plovers, snow buntings, snowy owls, and horned larks.

*Caribou, also known as reindeer, are among the main tundra animals, which also include musk ox, and arctic hares.*

## Boreal Coniferous Forests

As you continue your drive southward, you enter the great north woods biome, known by ecologists as the *boreal*, or northern, *coniferous forest*. Russians call it the *taiga*. It occupies a band running roughly from 57 degrees north to 45 degrees north, or from southern Alaska southward to Ottawa, Canada. Needle-leaf trees predominate, including different varieties of spruce, fir, and pine. But there are other kinds of trees as well, depending on whether you are west of the Rockies, in the

*The sprawling northern coniferous forest biome, commonly called the great north woods, extends southward to about 45 degrees north. Most of the trees are cone-bearing, such as spruce, fir, and pine, although white birches also are common. New York's northern forests border on this biome. The scene here, with numerous deciduous trees, is New York's Shawangunk Mountains.*

Midwest, or in the region of the Appalachians. One tree type, the jack pine, has a cone that remains tightly closed until there is a forest fire. Although the fire burns and sometimes kills seedlings and mature trees, scorched jack pine cones open, release their seeds, and can give rise to a new generation of pine trees and an entire new community. The eastern part of the biome contains a number of other trees including quaking aspen, balsam poplar, and paper birch. These too are stubborn survivors in the face of fire. New growth sprouts quickly from the destroyed trees' stumps and roots.

Mammals in this biome vary with latitude and include moose, bears, deer, wolverines, martens, lynx, sable, wolves, snowshoe hares, voles, chipmunks, shrews, and bats. The biome also supports numerous bird species—including robins, juncos, warblers, and nuthatches. There are only a few snakes and other reptiles and there are amphibians, especially in southern regions. And there are many insects, some of them pests—mosquitoes, blackflies, sawflies, and budworms—that attack people and vegetation alike.

## Temperate Deciduous Forests

Continuing your drive southward, you will enter the *temperate deciduous forest* biome. It sprawls southward from the Great Lakes all the way down to Florida and westward near the edge of Texas. This biome covers most of Europe, Japan, and much of southeast Asia. As you might imagine, climate is milder here than in the northern forests, and there is a much greater variety of trees, most of which are *deciduous*, meaning that they shed their leaves seasonally.

Tree types include oak, hickory, basswood, maple, beech, elm, willow, and sycamore. The eastern United States also has areas of white pine and red pine, both conifers. The ground cover is rich and diverse and includes many flowering plants.

*Deciduous trees predominate in the temperate deciduous forest biome, which in the east extends from the boreal coniferous forest border all the way southward to Florida. Ground cover includes many flowering plants.*

Typically, the ground-cover plants bloom quickly in the early spring before the trees come into leaf and keep the ground mostly in shade all summer. Compared with the heavily littered floor of the north woods, the forest floor in this biome is less cluttered with dead wood and other natural litter because of a more rapid rate of decomposition.

The largest animals that live in the part of this biome in the United States are deer and black bears. There used to be mountain lions and wolves until they were killed off by hunters or driven away. Smaller animals include foxes, bobcats, weasels, raccoons, squirrels, voles, and chipmunks. Birds include various woodpeckers, wild turkeys, grouse, and the red-eyed vireo. As we would expect from the warmer climate in these southern latitudes, many species of amphibians and reptiles are common.

*The ruffed grouse is among the many bird species of the temperate deciduous forest biome. Others include wild turkeys and woodpeckers.*

*The grasslands biome in central North America range from tall-grass prairie in the west to short-grass prairie in the east. The tall-grass prairie seen here is typical of South Dakota, for example. The Russians call their grasslands biome* steppes.

## Grasslands

If your biome exploration takes you due west from the Great Lakes and across to the Rocky Mountains, you will pass through miles and miles of the *grasslands* biome that covers much of central North America. In the eastern region are tall-grass prairies; in the west are the short-grass plains, typical of Nebraska with its buffalo grass. Russia's grasslands are known as *steppes*. South Americans call theirs *pampas*. Before agriculture became widespread in the eastern grasslands of North America, the region was densely covered by endless miles of blue-stem grass that grew to heights of 6.5 feet (2 meters). The soils of the tall-grass prairies are among the richest in the world due to the presence of rapidly decaying organic matter that collects in the upper layers. Forests, or rather clusters of trees, across the dry grasslands biome are pretty much restricted to valleys and streambanks. Generally, the climate becomes increasingly dry as you move westward.

*Short-grass prairie in the eastern range of the grasslands biome in the United States is typical of Nebraska with its buffalo grass. The South Americans call their grasslands biome* pampas.

Small burrowing mammals, including gophers, prairie dogs, squirrels, and jackrabbits are common and serve as prey for coyotes, wolves, and mountain lions. There also are pronghorn antelope, elk, badgers, ferrets, and bison. Grasslands birds include prairie chickens, longspurs, meadowlarks, hawks, and grasshopper sparrows. Before waves of settlers swept westward in the 1800s, an estimated 75 million bison grazed the western prairies. By 1888 fewer than a hundred survived the onslaught of human activity.

There are even more biomes, some covering smaller regions than those just portrayed, although each one has its own group of animals, bacteria, fungi, and soil nutrients that fuel their energy requirements. Each is a finely woven tapestry of varied life forms and intricate dependencies. However, by far the most precious and endangered of all these biomes are the tropical rain forests.

# Five

# Tragedy of the Rain Forests

Tropical rain forests are the planet's oldest, richest, and most diverse biological communities. They trace a green belt around the planet from about 30 degrees north to about 20 degrees south of the Equator. So many and so varied are the designs and behaviors of a tropical rain forest's plant and animal communities, and so bewildering their infinite interactions, that biologists who study the forests can feel overwhelmed. Millions of species make up the world's tropical rain forests. More woody plant species grow on one forested volcano in the Philippines than grow in the entire United States. Turn up two square feet of tropical rain forest leaf litter and fifty species of ants scurry out. For every human being there are some three-quarters of

*Like an undulating ocean, a tropical forest canopy, or roof, conceals the myriad growth and activity on the dark, moist floor far below. What remains of the world's tropical rain forests is fast disappearing, not to regrow to its present composition and structure for perhaps a million years. This scene is Soberania National Park, Panama.*

a ton of termites in the tropical rain forest biome. Amazonia has about 1,170 known bird species, but many more are still undiscovered. Central America has about 450 fish species, but there are more to be found. Compare those numbers with the total of about 190 fish species in all of Europe and only 172 in the Great Lakes. The number of species of tropical rain forest insects is unknown. They whir, whine, hum, and buzz with a million different voices. The diversity just among the palm trees of South American rain forests is staggering—more than 835 species.

The world's largest rain forest biomes are South America's Amazon basin, the East Indies (Sumatra, Borneo, and Papua New Guinea), and Africa's Congo basin. The global air circulation keeps these forests wet. Moist equatorial air rises from the forest canopy, is cooled aloft, condenses, and falls as rain. Meanwhile moist air is drawn in from the oceans and replaces the rising equatorial air.

Biologists are alarmed by the rapid loss and degradation of the rain forests by logging, slash-and-burn agriculture, and ranching, and little is being done to stop the destruction. Although numerous patches of national parks have been established, there is neither enough money nor park rangers to protect them. So illegal logging and land clearing continue. Biologists are concerned because of the loss of biodiversity. They are also just beginning to learn about the usefulness of rain forest plants as a source of drugs and medicines for a wide assortment of diseases.

## Medicinal Plants

English explorer Charles Waterton was one of the first Europeans to test a tropical rain forest plant's value as medicine, although rain forest people had relied on medicinal plants for thousands of years. Traveling in 1814 through what is now Guyana in South America, he witnessed the preparation of a poisonous substance the natives used to coat the tips of their arrows in order to kill game quickly. Curious about how the poison worked, he brought a sample back to London and injected some into a donkey. Within ten minutes the donkey stopped breathing, collapsed, and appeared dead. Waterton applied artificial respiration for two hours by pumping air through an opening he made in the donkey's windpipe. Within another two hours the donkey stood up and began walking around as if nothing had happened.

The mysterious substance was curare, the juice of a South American liana, or climbing plant. In weak doses it is safe to use as a muscle relaxant during certain delicate operations. But in strong doses curare completely relaxes muscles, including the diaphragm and heart, and results in death. In

*Throughout history people the world over have used hundreds of tropical rain forest plants as drugs to cure diseases and other ailments, to kill game with poisoned arrow tips, or to do in a political enemy with a poison brew. This exotic, nonpoisonous flower grows in the Amazon rain forest of South America.*

1541 the Spanish explorer Francisco de Orellana was dumbfounded when one of his men was struck in the finger by an arrow and died within a few minutes. A dose of another drug called physostigmine, which comes from a West African bean plant, quickly reverses the effects of curare, and it is useful for treating the *eye* disease glaucoma. Brazilian Indians of the Urueu-Wau-Wau tribe tip their arrows and spears with a poisonous sap squeezed from the red bark of the *tiki wha* tree. The sap prevents blood from forming clots and causes victims to bleed to death. Cancer researchers have long been interested in a class of chemicals, called alkaloids, found in tropical rain forest plants. About sixty alkaloids have been found in a single periwinkle plant of Madagascar, off Africa's southeast coast. Some are used to treat tumors, leukemia, and Hodgkin's disease. The National Cancer Institute has identified more than 2,000 tropical plants with anticancer properties. Botanists are convinced that there are many more tropical "miracle plants" awaiting discovery—if they can get to the plants before loggers, ranchers, and farmers cut the forests down.

## As the Forests Fall

Almost half the planet's rain forests have been shaved away. Every minute of the day and night nearly 150 acres (40 hectares) of rain forest fall to the chain saw or are recklessly destroyed by the bulldozer's blade. Many experts fear that most of the remaining rain forests will be gone by 2040. Thailand lost 45 percent of its rain forests between 1961 and 1985. In the Philippines the acreage of prized tall trees called dipterocarps shrank from 40 million in 1960 to one-sixteenth that much in the 1980s. The Philippines lost 55 percent of its rain forests in only 25 years. In Africa's Ivory Coast 75 percent of the forests were cut or burned over a 30-year period beginning in 1960. In Ghana, more than 80 percent of the forests have been cut or burned. In Brazil slash-and-burn farming has been causing an estimated loss of $2.5 billion a year. All of the primary rain forests in India, Bangladesh, Sri Lanka, and Haiti have been cut. According to the World Resources Institute, 30 million acres of tropical forest were destroyed in eight countries in 1987 alone.

A combination of logging, slash-and-burn farming, and land clearing by ranchers has brought disaster to the forests of Indonesia and Sabah, Malaysia. Cutting on watershed areas denudes the slopes. Instead of being buffeted by the plant cover and more slowly released into rivers and streams, rain hits the ground directly. The flood of downslope water then picks up soil, which flows into and clogs irrigation canals and floods inhabited lowland areas, driving people from their homes.

Many people who express concern over the rapid disappearance of the world's tropical rain forests suppose that most of the trees are harvested for use as timber. In fact, the reckless use of tractors and other logging equipment destroys 50 to 75 percent of the trees that are not cut. Such destruction has occurred in Sabah, Indonesia, and the Philippines. A logger carelessly cuts down a marked 120-foot dipterocarp, the only tree he is interested in. It comes crashing through the canopy and undergrowth, taking with it nine other trees. The nine other trees are left to rot. A bulldozer next smashes its way to the felled tree to cut a trail for the skidder that will haul the tree out to the road. Both bulldozer and skidder uproot, mangle, and otherwise destroy dozens more trees and churn the forest floor into mud. The manager on one logging operation in Indonesia said that his men take out only about four trees per acre. In the process the forest canopy is destroyed, and about one-sixth of the trees cut down for timber are so damaged that they are left behind to rot.

Slash-and-burn farming has become one of the leading causes of tropical rain forest destruction in the world. Every hour 50 acres (20 hectares) of rain forest are destroyed by this practice. Most of the burning flares up from the matches of land-poor settlers in Amazonia's Rondônia. In 1987 alone, 20 million acres of Rondônian forests went up in smoke.

The pressure to slash and burn is greatest in those countries where population growth is highest and, therefore, the demand for land greatest. Large numbers of Brazil's rain forest settlers have watched their dreams of becoming indepen-

*Only ugly scarring of the land is left after the logger's chain saw and the set-*
*tler's axe have turned once luxuriant forest into a wasteland. The world's trop-*
*ical rain forests, like this one in Papua, New Guinea, are fast disappearing as*
*the demand for land for farming and ranching increases with runaway world*
*population growth. Some experts fear that the remaining tropical rain forests*
*will be gone by the year 2040.*

dent farmers crumble. Because clearing a tropical forest is hard work, malaria and other parasitic diseases are rampant, and year after year of poor crop production is discouraging, many settlers of the virgin forest give up in despair. After only a few years the nutrient-poor forest soil is exhausted. Farmers either move and clear a new area, or they sell their land to wealthy cattle ranchers who live far away in the cities of São Paulo and Rio de Janeiro.

In Brazil more than six hundred cattle ranches average more than 50,000 acres (20,235 hectares) each. But the outlook for pastureland in a cleared forest is just as bleak as it is for farming. The settlers who sell their land often are kept on as paid laborers to further clear the land and plant grass for pasture. For a few years the grazing is good enough to support the cattle, which are ground up into hamburger meat for America's fast-food chains. After five or so years, weeds take over the pasture. Since clearing the weeds is too expensive, the land is once again abandoned, this time for good. Almost every ranch that was started in the Amazon before 1978 has been abandoned. That land will not see another tropical rain forest for a million years.

# Six

# Biodiversity: Going…Going…?

The world is now undergoing the fastest mass extinction in its entire history, according to seven out of ten biologists interviewed for a poll taken by the American Museum of Natural History in New York. The scientists said that the biodiversity loss the planet is now experiencing is more serious than global warming or pollution. One out of three of the scientists polled believe that half of all species now on Earth will die out by 2028. The survey is a "wake-up call" to all of us "that we are facing a serious threat not only to the health of the planet but also to humanity's own well-being and survival," says Ellen V. Futter, the museum's president.

*Gone forever. These extinct birds, called solitaries, were last seen in the 1750s on the island of Rodriguez in the Indian Ocean.*

# Habitat Loss and Extinction

No one will ever know the exact number of bird species wiped out by the Polynesians who colonized most of the 800 or so islands in the Pacific Ocean over the last 12,000 years. The Hawaiian Islands have lost some 60 ground-bird species since the Polynesians arrived between 900 and 500 years ago. Altogether, the Polynesians caused the extinction of around 2,000 bird species there. About 25 more species died out after 1778 when Europeans moved to the islands. Both groups destroyed bird habitats with the introduction of agriculture, pigs, rats, and dogs. Such extinctions are not isolated and rare events and they are not new in Earth's history. What is new is the rate at which numerous plant and animal species are becoming extinct. That rate is called the *background extinction rate*. The actual extinction rate is most likely hundreds or even thousands of times greater. From 1 to 10 species became extinct *every year*, on average, during the past 65 million years. In 1996 alone an estimated 1,000 to 10,000 species became extinct. Most extinctions today are due to loss of habitats due to human activity as the world population continues to soar. For example, there are about 100 million migrant people in the world today. That was the total world population at the time of classical Greek civilization. As forest biomes the world over are being carved up into ever smaller habitats, biodiversity suffers. Other extinctions are due to climate change, such as the warming oceans' destruction of coral reefs around the world.

One way habitats become lost is through a process called *fragmentation*. This occurs when forests are cut down for logging, road building, farms, or housing developments. Blocks of forest are made smaller and smaller, with many more barriers to species movement and dispersal. It has been described as an "ecological cancer" that eats away a forest section by section. Around the edge of each parcel, conditions are drier, hotter, and more windy than in the forest interior. The altered habitat conditions threaten both the plants and animals accustomed to moister, cooler, and dimmer conditions. It also kills off or forces species that need large territories for breeding and feeding to move. The resulting edge communities of plant and animals usually are much less diverse than the deep forest communities and can extend up to three-quarters of a mile (1.2 kilometers) into the forest interior. So a moist tropical forest need not be hacked to pieces to lose a significant amount of its biodiversity. Fragmentation can do the job nearly as effectively.

Logging of tropical forests in Brazil has eased since the 1960s. During the first half of the 1990s, some 356,000 acres (144,000 hectares) around Rio de Janeiro were logged, but in the second half of the decade only 8,650 acres (3,500 hectares) were lost. Just over one-third of eastern Brazil's remaining Atlantic rain forest today is officially protected, but only in a patchwork of 170 parks and other fragments. And because little is done to protect the parks, illegal logging goes on. In 1999, for instance, the mayor of a small Bahian city illegally logged 125 acres (50 hectares). Earlier, thousands of acres of prime forest, also in Bahia, were clear-cut to make room for eucalyptus plantations.

There is a general rule to estimate species extinctions due to habitat destruction. If 90 percent of a habitat is logged, we can expect 50 percent of all its species—from large animals to microscopic organisms—to become extinct. But critics of the rule say that there are too many uncertainties for it to be reliable as a species census taker. Some species will survive by migrating out of the area. And there is no way of knowing how long an extinction might take: ten years, fifty years, one hundred years?

## Extinctions Old and New

We know of five mass extinctions that have wiped out anywhere from 50 to 90 percent of all living things. And there may have been as many as twelve or more such periods, some caused when gigantic sheets of ice up to 2 miles (3 kilometers) thick covered parts of the planet. Other mass extinctions were caused by comets and asteroids smashing into the planet and filling the air with so much dust and debris that sunlight was seriously blocked and the lives of many animals and plants snuffed out. But characteristically, each time life recovered and bounced back, with millions of new species replacing those that could not adapt to the environmental changes that triggered the mass extinction and the wholesale loss of biodiversity. Such recoveries seem to take anywhere from five million to ten million years. If Earth is now heading into a sixth, and worst ever, period of mass extinction, we humans with our mushrooming world population may well be the cause.

**O**rdovician-Silurian Extinction, 439 million years ago—Probably caused by a lowering of the oceans because water became locked up as glacial ice and killed off numerous marine species. Later, sea levels rose as the glaciers melted and changed the environment again. Death toll: 85 percent of marine organisms.

# The Five Worst Extinctions in Earth's History

**Late Devonian Extinction, 364 million years ago**—Cause unknown. Death toll: about 80 percent of marine life. Nothing known about extinctions of life on land.

**Permian-Triassic Extinction, 251 million years ago**—Earth's worst mass extinction. A comet or asteroid strike may have been the culprit, causing massive outpourings of lava, enough to cover the entire planet to a depth of 10 feet (3 meters), but evidence for a cosmic hit has not been found. Some think the lava floods came from ruptures in the crust of what today is Siberia. Death toll: 90 percent of all sea life, along with 70 percent of land animals and most terrestrial plants.

**Triassic Extinction, 206 million years ago**—The most likely cause was massive floods of lava pouring out of what is now the Atlantic Ocean basin. Rocks from the eruptions have been found in the eastern United States, eastern Brazil, North Africa, and Spain. Deadly global warming may have followed and contributed to the extinctions. Death toll: more than 50 percent of all species were wiped out in less than 10,000 years, a mere tick on the geological clock.

**Cretaceous-Tertiary Extinction, 65 million years ago**—The famous extinction that is now thought to have contributed to the death of the dinosaurs. Strong evidence points to a major impact by a comet or asteroid. The impact created a gigantic crater—the Chicxulub Crater—in the floor of the Gulf of Mexico near Yucatan. Extensive lava flooding from what is now India is also suspected to have contributed to the mass extinctions. Death toll: up to 63 percent of marine organisms and about 20 percent of vertebrate animals living on land.

Scientists now think there may have been a total of one or two dozen mass extinctions over the last billion years, some caused or helped along by comet or asteroid strikes. These catastrophic strikes may also have set the stage for a burst of new plant and animal types following the impacts. The reason is that new and unoccupied ecological nooks and crannies were opened and competition among surviving species reduced in some cases.

# Extinction Crisis—Yes or No?

"How many kinds of plants and animals are there, Daddy?" asks the child. Daddy, who is a biologist, says he doesn't know. "How many kinds of plants and animals are dying out?" the concerned child asks next. "Now, we're in a better position to answer that," says the scientist. "At least, we can make some educated guesses by counting a certain species' populations today and comparing the count with reports of two or three hundred years ago."

Harvard University biologist Edward O. Wilson says we need to know three things to tell if there is a mass extinction crisis: first, the natural extinction rate; second, the current rate of extinction; and third, how fast the present rate seems to be speeding up. While a large number of biologists are convinced that it is speeding up and has reached a crisis, others aren't so sure. They say we really can't tell if there is an extinction crisis without knowing how many species there actually are.

Perhaps the question is too big to answer with confidence. We know relatively little about some plants and animals, though quite a lot about others. For example, we know birds pretty well. We now recognize nearly 10,000 bird species the world over. Each year, according to ecologist Stuart Pimm, two or three bird species become extinct while 11 to 14 percent are at risk. That rate of loss is about two hundred to three hundred times higher than past rates revealed by a study of the fossil record. Nevertheless, birds as a group worldwide seem to be among the least threatened. So, too, mammals, of which there are only about 4,810 species. We seem not to have lost a single mammal species in recent history, although some 25 percent are listed by the World Conservation Union (WCU) as endangered due to habitat fragmentation. And just as a new bird species pops up every now and then, so too

*The passenger pigeon, once abundant in the United States, is now extinct. Its gentle and fearless ways made the bird easy prey for hunters.*

does a new mammal species. Seven new monkey species have been reported in Brazil just since 1990.

The WCU's Red List of Threatened Wildlife lists a total of 5,205 species at risk, including 34 percent of fish, 25 percent of amphibians, and 20 percent of reptiles. Although these numbers might seem high, they do not prove that a mass extinction is now under way. Furthermore, the species counters point out that any single species' well-being or threatened status cannot be used as a measure of the health of all other species. Butterflies and pine trees respond to environmental change quite differently than a tropical forest monkey might. And so the argument continues between those who believe that mass extinctions are occurring and those who do not.

# Seven

# Today's Extinctions: Real, Imagined, or Exaggerated?

## Voices of Gloom

If it is not yet clear whether we are in the midst of the greatest mass extinction since the dinosaurs died out, then why are so many biologists in a state of gloom?

• According to Robert M. May, an Oxford University zoologist and former scientific adviser to the British government, the rate of species extinctions speeded up during the last one hundred years to about 1,000 times the rate before human beings evolved; and the rate probably will speed up 10 times faster over the next hundred years or so.

• According to Norman Myers, author of the 1979 book *The Sinking Ark*, 40,000 species die out each year.

• According to Edward O. Wilson, a leading authority on biodiversity, 1 to 10 percent of all species may die out every ten years, which amounts to at least 27,000 species a year.

• According to the American Museum of Natural History's Michael J. Novacek, we may have lost as much as 30 percent of all species by the mid-2000s.

These numbers can become confusing considering that different experts come up with numbers that often do not agree, from the total number of all species, to the natural—or background—rate of species extinctions, to the number of extinctions being caused by human activity. We may be driving living organisms to extinction at a rate of about a hundred species a day. If we assume a low total number of species of 10 million, that means that we are eliminating 0.2 to 0.6 percent of the planet's species every year.

As evidence of a serious decline in species, the voices of gloom point not only to the percentage of species considered threatened, but to species known to have become extinct. For instance, these scientists point out that the island of Madagascar has lost 17 of about 50 lemur species in the past 3,000 years, some as large as gorillas. In the past hundred years alone, 40 of about 950 fish species in North America have become extinct. Southern Africa has about 8,500 plant species found only in that region. Thirty-six have recently become extinct, and another 618 appear threatened. Worried scientists point out that such a rate of species loss is more rapid than replacement of new species by evolution, and hence means a rapid loss in biodiversity.

According to The Nature Conservancy's 1996 annual report, two-thirds of freshwater mussels have become extinct or are at risk. Freshwater fish, amphibians, and crayfish are close behind. Coral reefs in many parts of the world also seem to be in great danger.

# Mystery of the Disappearing Amphibians

Biologists are hard put to explain why recent years have seen a decline in frogs, toads, salamanders, and other amphibians in several parts of the world. Some point to pollution and others to habitat fragmentation. But even in many areas where habitats have remained healthy, amphibians have not.

Over the past 150 years Sri Lanka has lost 96 percent of its rain forest cover, and more than half its amphibians listed by naturalists before 1900 are no longer around. Some ecologists suspect that, in addition to habitat loss, habitat change may be the cause. Such change occurs when a forest of mixed vegetation is cut down and replaced by a plantation forest of only one species of trees. In Florida, flatwoods salamander populations declined over the years

*On the road to extinction? The golden toad, native to Coast Rica, was commonly seen in great numbers, but its populations have decreased markedly since 1987.*

as about 80 percent of the state's pine forests were cut and most replaced by a drier forest of commercial pine species. The salamanders do not do well in a dry forest habitat. In California some 75 percent of the tiger salamander's native grasslands habitat has been replaced by farmland and housing developments, with the result that the salamander is now on the endangered species list. In the Cascades Range of Oregon, even though the habitat of the Cascades frog and western toad have not been changed or polluted, the animals are disappearing. No one can say for sure why this is happening. In Costa Rica, 20 amphibian species have declined or disappeared just since the late 1980s. Among them is the famous golden toad.

Amphibians are a hardy lot and were the first land animals to evolve. They have been around for 350 million years and are found on every continent except Antarctica. Four northern species of frogs can freeze solid and survive. So far, biologists have identified some 5,000 species of amphibians. Yet some frogs are extremely sensitive and need just the right habitat conditions to maintain their populations. Some need a gently flowing stream at a certain water temperature and with a sandy bottom where they can lay their eggs.

The southeastern United States is the world's richest region in salamanders. Most species of salamanders do not have lungs and breathe through their skin, which must be kept moist at all times. When a forest is logged or wiped out, its salamander populations must move elsewhere or perish. Sunlight flooding the forest floor creates dry conditions that can spell death to salamanders. The favorite habitat of these skin-breathers are mature hardwood forests. At the present rate of cutting, the forests will be all but gone by 2010, and many salamander populations will also be gone. The great mystery is why amphibians in a variety of habitats—healthy, protected or those degraded by human activity—are dying out.

Some biologists think that pollution—acid rain, pesticides, herbicides, fertilizer runoff from farms—is eroding amphibian populations in many areas. The animals are especially sensitive to poisons that can easily penetrate their thin moist skin and their eggs, which lack protective shells.

Could a worldwide epidemic that seriously injures or kills off entire amphibian populations be involved? Some biologists think so, and they have identified the killer as chytrid fungus. Bacteria and viruses also seem to be agents of amphibian death in certain areas. Some biologists wonder if some disease agent that has spread worldwide is weakening amphibians' ability to fight off disease. In shallow lakes and ponds in western North America, climate change has reduced water level in many areas with high amphibian populations, especially of western toads. The result has been increased exposure of embryos to ultraviolet-B radiation, making them more sensitive to infection by disease agents. The eggs begin to develop normally for a few days but then turn white and die by the hundreds of thousands.

So where do all these local reports of frogs, salamanders, birds, fish, coral reefs, and other animals and their habitats leave us on a global basis? Are these simply local events that don't add

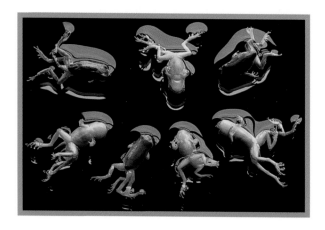

*An unusual number of mutations among certain amphibians have been reported in recent years, especially among frogs. Some frogs have been hatched with extra limbs, for example. Though the causes are still uncertain, such mutations may be caused by pesticide-polluted water where the amphibians breed, or by radiation.*

*Coral reefs are looked on as the rain forests of the oceans because of their rich biodiversity. Sixty-five percent of fish species live among the coral reefs. Yet, around the world, from the Caribbean to the Indian Ocean and Australia's Great Barrier Reef, more than one-quarter of the reefs are sick or dying. In some parts of the Pacific Ocean, the figure is 90 percent.*

up to a mass extinction? Some scientists say it may be too early to tell because the extinction of a species doesn't take place overnight. In some cases it may take ten years, in other cases a hundred or more. It's a hard question to answer.

Our lack of detailed knowledge about how many species there are on the planet and how they are distributed makes some scientists cautious about estimating the number of species now headed for extinction and about how fast others are headed there. Nevertheless, there is agreement among scientists that species appear to be fading out at an unnaturally high rate. In 1995 one thousand scientists from more than fifty countries agreed. In a report called *Global Biodiversity Assessment,* the scientists asserted that species are becoming extinct at fifty to one hundred times the natural (background) expected rate. In the Pacific region, bird species are dwindling at one thousand times the natural rate.

## A Voice of Doubt

Mention the name Bjørn Lomborg and most ecologists wince. Lomborg is a professor of mathematics at the University of Aarhus, Denmark. In his book, *The Skeptical Environmentalist*, he says that the world is not nearly in as much danger as many environmentalists claim, and that their voices of gloom about mass extinction have vastly overstated biodiversity losses.

Lomborg argues that Myers's 1979 claim that 40,000 species become extinct each year, or one hundred species a day, is nonsense. It is, he says, 10,000 times greater than the latest observed rate of extinctions. Nevertheless, he adds, that the figure of 40,000 has been unquestioningly accepted by "millions of people the world over." He also states that reasons for preserving the world's rain forests have been twisted. He cites biologist Thomas Lovejoy, who says that a large number of all species live in tropical rain forests. Leave the rain forests alone, and nothing will happen to any of the species. Cut down the rain forests, and most species will disappear. Lomborg then quotes Lovejoy as claiming that if half the tropical forests are cut down, one-third of all their species will disappear.

If that notion is true, Lomborg then asks, "Just what do we lose?" Many people immediately think of elephants, leopards, apes, and mahogany trees. He then points out that 95 percent of tropical forest species are beetles, ants, flies, microscopic worms, fungi, and bacteria. Furthermore, he says that if one parcel of rain forest is cleared, many animals and plants simply carry on in neighboring forest areas. For instance, 99 percent of Puerto Rico's primary forests were cut over a period of 400 years. During that time 7 out of 60 bird species became extinct, but today the island has 97 bird species. "Our mistake is to believe that all cleared rainforest is simply razed and left barren," Lomborg says. He then adds that about half of all tropical forest that is cleared turns into secondary forest.

Lomborg comes down hard on biologist Edward O. Wilson's rule of thumb that if a forest area is reduced by 90 percent, the number of species will be halved. Originally, Wilson meant the rule to apply to island communities where there are no other locations to be occupied by a threatened species, but the rule cannot be applied to large continental regions, says Lomborg. He then cites the destruction of 88 percent of Brazil's Atlantic rain forest, with only fragmented areas left. According to Wilson's rule, half of all the forest's species should have become extinct. However, the Brazilian Society of Zoology could not find "a single known animal or plant species that had become extinct." In fact, "an appreciable number" of species considered extinct twenty years ago, according to the society's report, have cropped up, including several bird species and six butterfly species. Lomborg points out that "we demand that developing countries stop chopping down their forests even though we have eradicated about 99 percent of our own primary forest."

He concludes by insisting that the widely quoted species loss rate of 40,000 a year is a figure that cannot be shown to be in agreement with observed species loss rates. Lomborg claims that the planet's forest cover has expanded since 1950. The United Nations Forest Resources Assessment says that the world actually lost 4.2 percent of its natural forests during the

1990s alone. Lomborg claims that "marine productivity has almost doubled since 1970." He says that biodiversity loss will be "0.7 percent over the next 50 years." E. O. Wilson claims the figure will be at least ten times higher. Lomborg's controversial book has drawn severe criticism from many environmental scientists. Some have called the book a fraud and a distorted attack written by a non-scientist who used out-of-date information and twisted real facts beyond recognition. The result has been confusion among the public and the politicians whose job it is to write environmental regulations. Wilson concludes: "My greatest regret about the Lomborg scam is the extraordinary amount of scientific talent that has to be expended to combat it in the media."

Even though it is often hard to get various groups of scientists to agree on the numbers of species that appear to be going extinct, or on the overall rate of species loss, all, including Lomborg, agree on at least four things that point to a crisis in biodiversity loss on a global basis:

• Habitat loss or degradation endangers species by reducing their populations.
• Logging, agricultural expansion, ranching, housing, and industrial development continue to erode and fragment land habitats.
• A combination of overfishing, the pollution of marine habitats, and rising ocean temperatures due to global warming are dangerously reducing the populations of many aquatic species.
• The adverse effects of human activity on an ever-increasing scale, due to our out-of-control population growth, is the cause of habitat loss and destruction the world over.

# Eight

# Gaia

## Gaia and the Very End

Gaia was the Greek goddess of Earth. The British chemist James Lovelock in 1974 adopted Gaia's name for his theory about a relationship between Earth and its myriad diverse life forms. He believes that the two share a close biological union. Each affects the other's well-being in a living association called *symbiosis*. As Lovelock was developing his ideas, he was joined by the American biologist Lynn Margulis.

Gaia theory is that Earth's realm of biodiversity largely keeps the planet more or less the way it is, capable of supporting life. Despite ice ages that have piled up 2-mile-(3.2-kilometer) thick layers of ice over large parts of the planet, and despite numerous peltings by comets and asteroids that have wiped out millions of species, the planet has remained habitable for nearly four billion years. Although untold millions of species have come and gone, the great chain of life has not once been broken. Gaia is the union of three things: all the organisms and ecosystems that have ever existed; Earth itself, with its oceans, atmosphere, and rocks; and the Sun as a source of energy.

According to Lovelock, life controls and maintains conditions on the planet. It does so by responding to changes in climate and all other workings of the environment. It then regulates certain parts of the environment to best suit its needs. Recall that Earth's early atmosphere was very different from the air we breathe today. The oxygen revolution did not just happen. It was brought on by living matter that learned how to carry out photosynthesis. While some of the planet's primitive organisms were poisoned by the massive buildup of atmospheric oxygen, others found it a better way to carry out life's many chemical reactions. Once the oxygen level reached about 21 percent of the total atmosphere, it stopped accumulating and has remained just about the same ever since. Why? According to Gaian thinking, living organisms are maintaining that level. If the level increased only a few percent, the forests would burst into flame by spontaneous combustion. If it decreased only a few percent, there would be widespread death of many oxygen users.

Some scientists feel uncomfortable with the Gaia theory. They say it's too fuzzy, that it can't be measured or tested, and that it is too "unscientific." Others feel that it's at least an interesting way to view Earth.

## The Long Road Ahead

Throughout all of Earth's geologic history, the ceaseless twisting, churning, flooding, and drying of the land, the spewing of ash, dust, and gases into the atmosphere by volcanoes, and the repeated grinding of massive glaciers have shaped and reshaped the land and seas and altered global climate again and again. Those geological forces also directed the countless avenues of success and dead-end alleys that the world's stunning variety of plants and animals have taken.

To this day evolution continues, and it will continue until the Sun dies a few billion years from now. No one can say what species may still be around then or what new ones will have come and gone before the Sun burns itself out, as it must when it uses up its hydrogen fuel. But that time is further into the future than the origins of life on Earth are back in the past. In the meantime, who can tell what strange and marvelous life forms will appear on our planet and for a few billion years enjoy their place in the Sun as we are now enjoying ours?

*Pictured are two primate species: the Colobus monkey (left) and the Golden Tamarin monkey (below). Primates include humans, apes, monkeys, lemurs, and tarsiers. A number of primate species, including several populations of humans, are facing hard times with a bleak future. According to the World Conservation Union, nearly half of all primates are now threatened with extinction. Habitat loss and degradation by human activity are the major causes.*

# Glossary

**Background extinction**—the rate of extinction typical of the fossil record.

**Biodiversity**—the total variation among all living organisms, including their genetic makeup and habitats.

**Biome**—a large regional ecosystem such as desert, grasslands, great north woods, and tropical rain forests.

**Boreal coniferous forest**—that biome of cone-bearing trees between 57 degrees north and 45 degrees north, such as the great north woods and the taiga.

**Canopy**—the leafy "roof" of a forest.

**Carnivore**—any organism that eats meat.

**Closed ecological system**—an ecosystem that is self-sufficient and self-contained except for the input of energy from the Sun.

**Cold-blooded**—organisms, such as reptiles, whose body temperature fluctuates with changes in the temperature of the environment.

**Community**—a localized mixture of plants and animals living together.

**Cosmic year**—a 240-million-year cycle, the time it takes the Sun and its planets to make one complete trip around the center of the Milky Way galaxy.

**Cyanobacteria**—blue-green primitive algae that have survived over millions of years of evolution.

**Deciduous**—trees that shed their leaves seasonally.

**Ecosystem**—the living and nonliving parts of the environment that together produce a unique system—such as a desert, the tundra, or grasslands, but also more specific than a biome.

**Fragmentation**—carving up an ecosystem, such as forest, into ever smaller units, with the result that the range of habitats shrinks, resulting in species loss.

**Genus**—a classification category ranking below a family and above a species, generally consisting of several species.

**Grasslands**—that biome in which the dominant plants are grasses. In the eastern region of the midwestern United States tall-grass prairies predominate; in the western region are the short-grass plains.

**Habitat**—any area where all the needs of a given population of plants or animals are provided.

**Herbivore**—any organism that depends on plants as its food supply.

**Hotspot**—a region of especially high biodiversity, such as Brazil's Atlantic rain forest where many forest communities are disappearing very rapidly.

**Mutant**—any organism that has undergone a mutation.

**Mutation**—a change in one or more genes that causes an offspring to differ in one or more ways from its parents.

**Natural selection**—the process by which those individuals who are the fittest, or best adapted to environmental conditions, survive and reproduce.

**Pampas**—a South American term for grasslands.

**Permafrost**—permanently frozen ground.

**Photosynthesis**—a green plant's ability to make the sugar, glucose, by combining carbon dioxide and water in the presence of sunlight.

**Species**—a classification category ranking below a genus and consisting of a group of organisms capable of interbreeding.

**Steppes**—a Russian term for grasslands.

**Symbiosis**—a relationship of organisms of different species, usually in close physical contact for mutual interdependence.

**Taxonomy**—that branch of science concerned with the classification of organisms.

**Tundra**—that far northern biome of shrubs and sedges circling the globe southward down to about 60 degrees north latitude.

**Warm-blooded**—organisms, such as mammals, with the ability to regulate their body temperature at a more or less constant level.

# Further Reading

Abramovitz, Janet N. *Imperiled Waters, Impoverished Future: The Decline of Freshwater Ecosystems*. World Watch Paper 128 (1996).

Abrams, Peter A. *The Unified Neutral Theory of Biodiversity and Biogeography*. Princeton, NJ: Princeton University Press, 2001.

Ayres, Ed. "The Fastest Mass Extinction in Earth's History." *World Watch* (September/October 1998), pp. 6–7.

Baskin, Yvonne. "Ecologists Dare to Ask: How Much Does Diversity Matter?" *Science* (April 8, 1994), pp. 202–203.

Becker, Luann. "Repeated Blows." *Scientific American* (March 2002), pp. 76–83.

Bright, Chris, and Ashley Mattoon. "The Restoration of a Hotspot Begins." *World Watch* (November/December 2001), pp. 8–16.

Brown, Lester, et al. *State of the World 2001*. Washington, DC: Worldwatch Institute, 2001.

Daily, Gretchen C. "Ecological Forecasts." *Nature* (May 17, 2001), p. 245.

Gallant, Roy A. *Earth's Vanishing Forests*. New York: Macmillan, 1991.

———. *The Origins of Life*. Tarrytown, NY: Marshall Cavendish, 2001.

Gibbs, W. Wayt. "On the Termination of Species." *Scientific American* (November 2001), pp. 40–49.

Kiesecker, Joseph M., Andrew R. Blaustein, and Lisa K. Belden. "Complex Causes of Amphibian Population Declines." *Nature* (April 5, 2001), pp. 468–469.

Lomborg, Bjørn. *The Skeptical Environmentalist*. Cambridge, England: Cambridge University Press, 2001.

Margulis, Lynn. *Symbiotic Planet*. New York: Basic Books, 1998.

Mattoon, Ashley. "Amphibia Fading." *World Watch* (July/August 2000), pp. 12–23.

Morell, Virginia. "The Variety of Life." *National Geographic* (February 1999), pp. 7–31.

Pimm, Stuart L. *The World According to Pimm*. New York: McGraw-Hill, 2001.

Pounds, J. Alan. "Climate and Amphibian Declines." *Nature* (April 5, 2001), pp. 639–640.

Rothschild, Lynn J., and Rocco L. Mancinelli. "Life in Extreme Environments." *Nature* (February 22, 2001), pp. 1092–1101.

Ryan, John C. *Life Support: Conserving Biological Diversity*. World Watch Paper 108 (1992).

Schmidt, Karen. "Life on the Brink." *Earth* (April 1997), pp. 26–33.

Schubert, Charlotte. "Life on the Edge: Will a Mass Extinction Usher in a World of Weeds and Pests?" *Science News* (September 15, 2001), pp. 168–170.

Tuxill, John. *Nature's Cornucopia: Our Stake in Plant Diversity*. World Watch Paper 148 (September 1999).

————. "Death in the Family Tree." *World Watch* (September/October 1997), pp. 13–21.

Ward, Geoffrey C. "India's Western Ghats." *National Geographic*, (January 2002), pp. 90–109.

Wilson, E. O. ed. *Biodiversity*. Washington: National Academy Press, 1988.

# Index

Page numbers for illustrations are in **boldface**.

# About the Author

**Roy A. Gallant**, called "one of the deans of American science writers for children" by *School Library Journal*, is the author of almost one hundred books on scientific subjects, including the National Geographic Society's *Atlas of Our Universe*. Among his other books are *When the Sun Dies*; *Earth: The Making of a Planet*; *Before the Sun Dies*; *Earth's Vanishing Forests*; *The Day the Sky Split Apart*, which won the 1997 John Burroughs award for nature writing; and *Meteorite Hunting*, a collection of accounts about his expeditions to Siberia to document major meteorite impact crater events. His most recent award is a lifetime achievement award presented to him by the Maine Library Association.

From 1979 to 2000, (professor emeritus) Gallant was director of the Southworth Planetarium at the University of Southern Maine. He has taught astronomy there and at the Maine College of Art. For several years he was on the staff of New York's American Museum of Natural History and a member of the faculty of the museum's Hayden Planetarium. His specialty is documenting on film and in writing the history of major Siberian meterorite impact sites. To date, he has organized eight expeditions to Russia and is planning his ninth, which will take him into the Altai Mountains near Mongolia. He has written articles about his expeditions for *Sky & Telescope* magazine and for the journal *Meteorite*. Professor Gallant is a fellow of the Royal Astronomical Society of London and a member of the New York Academy of Sciences. He lives in Rangeley, Maine.